TAK KUBOTA'S
FIGHTING KARATE

TAK KUBOTA'S
FIGHTING KARATE

TAKAYUKI KUBOTA

DISCLAIMER: Please note that the author and publisher of this book are NOT RESPONSIBLE in any manner whatsoever for any injury that may result from practicing the techniques and/or following the instructions given within. Since the physical activities described herein may be too strenuous in nature for some readers to engage in safely, it is essential that a physician be consulted prior to training.

First Revised Edition published in 2022 by AWP LLC/Empire Books.

Copyright © 2022 by AWP LLC/Empire Books. All rights reserved. No part of this publication may be reproduced or utilized in any form or by any means, electronic or mechanical, including photo- copying, recording, or by any information storage and retrieval system, without prior written permission from AWP LLC/Empire Books.

EMPIRE BOOKS P.O. Box 491788, Los Angeles, CA 90049

First Revised Edition Library of Congress Catalog Number: ISBN-13: 978-1-949753-44-8

22. 21 20 19 18 17 16 15 14 13 12 11 10

Library of Congress Cataloging-in-Publication Data:

Tak Kubota's Fighting Karate / by Tak Kubota -- Revised ed. p. cm.
ISBN 978-1-949753-44-8 (pbk. : alk. paper) 1. Karate. 5. Martial arts--technique.
3. Large type books. I. Title. GV1114.3.F715 20148861.815'3--dc22
2006013422

PRINTED IN THE UNITED STATES OF AMERICA

Acknowledgments

The following people assisted Soke Tak Kubota in the preparation of this book: Shihan Ted Bratakos, Shihan Val Mijailovic, Shihan Adam Pearson, Shihan Tatsuo Hirano, Shihan Rod Kuratomi, Shihan George Rolon, Shihan Dai Norvell Carrere, Sensei Andre Artuni, Sensei Leigh Foad, and Senior Shihan Hank Hamilton.
 — IKA Gosoku Ryu Founder and Grandmaster
 Soke Takayuki Kubota, 10th Dan

International Karate Association
World Headquarters
3301 N. Verdugo Rd.
Glendale, CA 91208 U.S.A.
Web site: www.ikakarate.com
(818) 541-1240

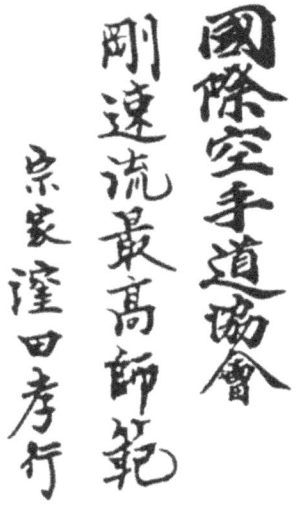

Contents

What is Gosoku Ryu? — By Hank Hamilton 9
Gosoku Ryu World Champions 17
What Others Are Saying About Tak Kubota 19
IKA Glossary 25
    Parts of the Body 27
    Numbers 27
    Belt Rankings 27
    Black Belt 28
    Titles 28
    Stances 28
    Strikes 29
    Kicks 31
    Blocks 31
IKA Honbu No Kata 33
    Gosoku Ryu 33
    Shotokan 33
    Gosoku Weapons Kata 33
    Kubota Jiu-Jitsu 34

Gosoku Ryu Forms, Training Exercises, and Techniques

Kicking Form 36

Tsuki Kata (Punching Form) 40

Uke Kata (Blocking Form) 45

Training Exercises for Geri and Tsuki Kata 54

Arm and Focus Training 58

Balance Training 62

Makiwara and Hammer Training 64

Kumite Fighting Form 68

Waza (Technique) 72

Geri (Kicking) 140

Nage Waza 170

AGAINST THE GRAIN--
An Interview with Master Kubota 191

Pictured are some of grandmaster Kubota's World Champions. In first row from left: Shihan Hirano Tatsuo, Sensei Leigh Foad, Shihan George Rolon, and Grandmaster Tak Kubota (standing).
In top row from left: Shihan Rod Kuratomi, Andre Artuni, Shihan Dai Norvell Carrere, Shihan Adam Pearson, and Shihan Ted Bratakos.

What Is Gosoku Ryu?

By Hank Hamilton

Gosoku Ryu karate is a phenomenon in the world of martial arts in that it was created by a small teen-age boy living in abject poverty in early post-war Tokyo, and grew to be the most widely accepted style of Japanese karate in the world.

At the age of 15, Takayuki Kubota also began teaching the Kamata division of the Tokyo Police Department his own created defensive and apprehending techniques. These have long been in demand by law enforcement around the world. To date, grandmaster Kubota has trained over 800 police departments, agencies, and bureaus.

The World Discovers Gosoku Ryu
Consisting of several intricate kata (multi-move forms) and myriad awesome attack and defense techniques, it is no wonder so many outstanding instructors and practitioners worldwide have rededicated themselves to the Gosoku style. Kubota's International Karate Association (IKA) now has dojo in many U.S. cities, as well as 52 foreign countries.

Having read of the exploits of Takayuki Kubota (he was also used by the Tokyo Police Department as a one-man riot control), I was shocked and pleased to see a small dojo in Hollywood with his name on the door. The year was 1965, and as a karate devotee since childhood, I had been quite impressed by accounts of this Japanese legend.

Loud thumps, kiais, moans and thuds accompanied my climb up the narrow stairs. At their top I found a room, barren except for an immaculate hardwood floor and four large men attacking one small man, all in white karate gis. One of the large men wore a brown belt; the other three wore black.

The smaller man wore a worn black belt with a red interior. He was gleefully punching, kicking and slamming to the floor each of the men as though they were rag dolls.

Heavy Hitters
The three black belts were Tonny Tulleners, Harvie Eubanks and Ben Otake. The brown belt was the late John Gehlson. During a brief break in the action, Tonny passed me on the way to the water fountain and muttered, "I'm 6-foot-2 of bruise."

Tonny had been with the late karate virtuoso Ed Parker and was already building an international reputation winning tournaments; Ben was one of the chief instructors for Parker. Harvie, trained in Japan, was a Los Angeles Police Department sergeant and chief defensive tactics instructor at the L.A. Police Academy; and John was a young, tough street cop who had found his hero in Kubota.

All had first met Shihan (master) Kubota on his first visit to the U.S. as Ed Parker's headliner guest demonstrator at Ed Parker's famed Long Beach Internationals in 1963. (The third name listed on that marquee of demonstrators was a Chinese martial artist named Bruce Lee.) When Kubota moved the headquarters of his fledgling IKA, as well as himself, to Los Angeles, John Gehlson became his first student. He was quickly followed by Harvie, Ben and Tonny.

John became such a disciple to Kubota and his teachings that he moved into the dojo and spent every off-duty hour training with the master. Since the dojo had no shower at that time, both took care of such things daily as the guests of Sgt. Eubanks at the L.A. Police Academy.

Workout and Punishment
Regular classes were an hour and a half of grueling workout and punishment, featuring Kubota's Japanese ethic of "little touch okay." But Shihan's science was so outstanding and gratifying that many of us would arrange to attend two classes a day, plus a noon class on Saturdays. Gehlson kept on in between!

It wasn't long before John had his black belt and became a real nemesis to the superstars of that era, including Tulleners. In fact, it became a tandem which found one winning the finals in almost every major tournament. They were the same size: Tonny was blond, John had dark hair. Rather a positive/negative competition.

Like Shihan Kubota, not all his disciples were large, but also like him, they had dedication, a natural charisma, and either had or developed a great sense of humor. Among the immortals was fun-loving, very personable Ron Glaubitz. Compared to the 6-2s of Gehlson and Tulleners, and the former "Mr. California," Harvie Eubanks, Ron was small at around 5-foot-8. But he was a

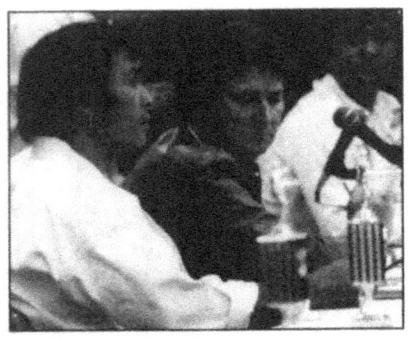

dynamo at kumite and a great technician in kata.

Eventually, he saw a need for an IKA in Mexico, so he moved south and opened a dojo in Tijuana and later in Rosarito Beach. There, he trained quite a few continuing disciple-instructors, such as the Pedraza brothers, Sydney and Dante, and long-time black belt Yolanda McCausland, widow of another IKA great, the late Ron McCausland.

A New Chapter
This brings up another chapter in the early IKA-USA saga. An independant karate instructor named Griffin had a small, but very promising, entourage of black belt students in Monrovia, Calif. He brought them to a class at Shihan Kubota's new headquarters, located at Hollywood boulevard and Kenmore avenue, in Hollywood. They were so impressed they decided to come on a regular basis. As has always been Kubota's policy, you have to prove yourself qualified as an IKA black belt to wear one at his dojo. Therefore, the new contingent, including its sensei, Griffin, returned to white belts. Eventually Griffin dropped out, but the others, Ron McCausland, Kenny ("Little Tarzan") Kuch, George Byrd and Bill Jubb, all rose quickly back to black belts and established themselves as Hall-of-Fame members of the IKA.

It was at the Hollywood and Kenmore dojo when, one afternoon, a lovely, shy

young lady from the Midwest, accompanied by her girlfriend, came in and signed up for regular classes. They both applied themselves quite well, but eventually the girlfriend dropped out. The other, Thea, did so well she eventually married the grandmaster.

It was also at that dojo where one of Kubota's top students from Japan rejoined him. Takemas Okuyama brought a new "eat 'em up alive", "never back up" dedication to the IKA headquarters. Okuyama has now established IKA as the dominant martial arts force in Canada.

Ben Otake later introduced Kubota's Gosoku Ryu to Puerto Rico, and IKA still flourishes in the exotic islands of the Caribbean under the tutelage of Shihan Manuel Gonzales. Hawaii became the quest and accomplishment of IKA veteran and now active regular headquarters instructor, Ted Bratakos.

Superstar Style
Many superstars of the martial arts world got their beginnings at the Hollywood boulevard and Kenmore avenue venue of the IKA World Headquarters. Among the most outstanding were the Mijailovic brothers, Vladan and Dragan. Val, as he is now known worldwide, was a gigantic junior at Hollywood High; his brother, Dragan, was a senior at the same school. Their dedication to pain and progress caused a meteoric

rise for them in the most prestigious tournaments throughout the world.

The Mijailovics were from Yugoslavia, but they grew up in the U.S. Boban Petkovic, a fellow Yugoslavian who competed in an IKA tournament while touring with a national dance troop, was so impressed with Kubota's warriors and the shihan's techniques that he decided to defect from the then-Communist Bloc.

For several years, the coveted IKA championships were swapped back and forth between "Baby Huey" Val and the "Bad Boy from the Balkans," Boban.

There is an abundance of champions and future champions currently active at the headquarters; far too many to acknowlege, but two bear mention here. These two outstanding young men, who have grown up under the Kubota guidance and currently win just about every competition, both in citizenship and combat, are Tyler Kubota (heir to the throne) and Rod Kuratomi.

Because of the spectacular success of Gosoku Ryu, the original style of karate created by So-Shihan Kubota, and its acceptance and expansion to dojo worldwide, the Ministry of Education in Japan has bestowed the coveted title of Soke (founder of a style) on him. This makes him the only living holder of such a title in the world.

"Go Fast"

Like shotokan, shito, goju, shorin, tae kwon do, and tang soo, Gosoku is a complete style composed of many special techniques and kata. The name itself describes why it is unique to martial arts: "Go" means "strong" and "Soku" means "fast." The inventive mind of Soke Kubota combined the blazing speed that comes from the softness of most Chinese styles with the massive power of Japanese techniques. To these he has added elements of aikido, judo and jiu-jitsu to create a near-invincible, easily learned martial art for maximum protection on the street and judge-pleasing performance in tournaments.

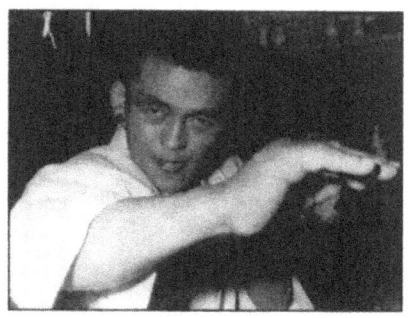

Nothing breeds success like success. And the wide-reaching praises of Soke Kubota's many successes have drawn other great instructors and masters into his fold. A great example is Dr. Tatsuo Hirano. Shihan Hirano's quiet dominance in the arts and articulate teaching techniques provide a very solid platform for the advancement of many upcoming IKA stars.

Any history of IKA in the U.S. would be incomplete without the acknowledgement of our own soke-dai and associate to Soke Kubota, the character-driven actor and dedicated Kubota disciple/student/instructor for the past 30 years, James "Jimmie" Caan.

The martial arts is not the only "arts" soke Kubota has mastered. He has also made himself well-known and accepted in

the entertainment arts, having been featured in more than 299 movies and TV shows, and over 186 TV commercials. In fact, at one time Caan (jokingly) said if Kubota didn't quit doing so many movies, he was going to start a karate association!

It would take a multipage manuscript to list all the stellar family of the IKA headquarters alone, but let's end with a partial listing of many who have received so much from, and contributed so much to, Soke Takayuki Kubota and his Kokusai Karate-do Kyokai (International Karate Association): Leonard Kramer, Paul McCaul, Dennis Loeb, Rod Pattersan, Miguel Lopez, Tom Sadowski, Isamu Manako, Tom Fukashima, Herbert Wright, Norvell Carrere, Raffi Kurdian, Judy Marx, Ralph Bailey, Fernando Grimaldo, Antonio Antonetti, Adam Pearson, and Ron McClauslan.

And though not officially located at the headquaters dojo, these IKA family members also have always been of great support: Pasadena's Adam Pearson and Tom Serrano; Alaska's Charles Scott and Richard Isley; San Jose (Calif.'s) Jim Mather; and Australia's (officially knighted) Sir Tewamoana Terupe, chief of IKA South Pacific.

Gosoku Ryu World Champions

Following is a list of World Champions trained in Gosoku Ryu from 1964–2002 by Soke Takayuki Kubota.

Tonny Tulleners
John Gehlsen
Harvie Eubanks
Ron McCauslan
Ralph Bailey
Ted Bratakos
Ron Glaubitz
David Vaughn
George Byrd
Greg Pickerell
Manuel Gonzales
Isamu Manako
Val Mijailovic
Boban Petkovic
Miguel Lopez
Tom Sadowski
Kenny Kuch
Yuzo Hirachi
Yolanda McCausland

Tom Serrano
Dragan Mijailovic
Dave White
George Sinani
Rod Kuratomi
George Rolon
Bill Bon
Tony Ponterelli
Adam Pearson
Paul McCaul
Leigh Foad

Current IKA Tournament Coaches
Soke Takayuki Kubota
Shihan Ted Bratakos

IKA Headquarters Instructor
Shihan Tatsuo Hirano

WHAT OTHERS ARE SAYING ABOUT TAK KUBOTA

Even before the world became aware of any Asian martial art other than judo, those who gained fame in physical combat sports knew of the genius and prowess of young Takayuki Kubota. Long before his first visit to the U. S., Tak Kubota had been visited at his small dojo in Tokyo by world-famous judoka, professional wrestler and movie stunt coordinator, Gene LeBell.

In 1963, karate grandmaster and entrepeneur Ed Parker, recognizing young Kubota's charisma and expertise, financed the master's first trip to the Los Angeles area to be featured as the special guest demonstrator at his Long Beach Internationals.

So impressive were Shihan (Master) Kubota's demonstrations at the tournament and later at the Los Angeles Police Academy, he was deluged with requests from karate enthusiasts and police department executives to move his dojo to Southern California. He would make the move a year later.

Thirty-six years later, to celebrate his 60 years in karate and the Millennium, he presented his "10th Kubota World Cup Karate Championship" in Los Angeles. This three-day event drew over 2,000 karate competitors from 52 countries, as well as letters of congratulations from some of the most-influential leaders in the world. Here's what they had to say:

Bill Clinton, former president of the United States:
"Warm greetings to the participants, coaches, and spectators gathered for the tenth Kubota World Cup Karate Championship. I commend each of the competitors for your

deep personal commitment to excellence, and I extend best wishes to all for a rewarding experience."

Al Gore, former vice president of the United States:
"...I want to congratulate Grandmaster Takayuki Kubota on his six decades in the martial arts and the International Karate Association on their 36th Anniversary."

Dianne Feinstein, U.S. senator from California:
"Your volunteer work training law enforcement officers in the art of karate has been an asset to the community and your future efforts are encouraged."

Barbara Boxer, U.S. senator from California:
"Your extraordinary expertise in the martial arts field should make this an exciting and inspiring tournament for all those in attendance."

Gray Davis, governor of California:
"On behalf of the State of California, I extend best wishes for continued success."

Benjamin J. Cayetano, former governor of Hawaii:
"Tenth-degree black belt and president and founder of the International Karate Association, grandmaster Kubota has

trained some of the world's most-respected military forces and law enforcement agencies over the past six decades."

James E. Rogan, former U.S. congressman and assistant majority whip:
"Grandmaster Kubota has been an outstanding role model and mentor for helping keep our youth physically and mentally healthy."

The Board of Supervisors of the County of Los Angeles:
"With sincere congratulations and best wishes, the Board of Supervisors of the County of Los Angeles does hereby join in your celebration."

Richard J. Riordan, former mayor of Los Angeles:
"The City is also grateful for the countless hours of training you have given to officers of the Los Angeles Police Department and for the techniques that you have developed which help them do their jobs more safely and effectively."

Russell K. Silverling, chief of police, Glendale, Calif.:
"As so many of our officers can attest, the intensity, dedication, and excellence of your training philosophy will certainly be demonstrated through your many students from around the world..."

Ted Cooke, chief of police, Culver City, Calif.:
"You have been so important in the teaching of baton techniques, but also teaching the proper attitude when dealing with physical contact."

Stacey Murphy, mayor, Burbank, Calif:
"On behalf of Burbank's Chief of Police and myself, I would like to thank you for your tremendous dedication and commitment in educating and training law enforcement officers of the Burbank Police Department as well as those of surrounding jurisdictions."

Walter M. Saiton, president of the Japanese Cultural Center of Hawaii:
"It is remarkable to note that grandmaster Kubota has trained many esteemed departments and agencies worldwide, such as the Tokyo P.D., the F.B.I., the U.S. Army Military Police, and other outstanding law enforcement agencies."

Satoru Toyoda, president of Nanka Kumamoto Kenjinkai:
"I and all the members of Nanka Kumamoto Kenjinkai are very proud of you, Mr. Kubota, for your endless efforts in spreading your unique style of karate do throughout the world."

Arnold Schwarzenegger, Hollywood box-office superstar:
"I have long known of your excellence in martial arts. Your constant training of police departments and agencies worldwide is legendary."

James Caan, famous Hollywood actor:
"Of the many exciting and unusual experiences I have had, the weeks of assisting you in training the 'street cops' of the Culver City Police Department in hand-to-hand defensive and street tactics rank among the most memorable and enjoyable. After all, how often can you beat up on a cop and have him thank you?"

INTERNATIONAL KARATE ASSOCIATION GLOSSARY

General

Arigato—Thank you
Budo—Martial arts (collective)
Bunkai—Analysis or breakdown of kata moves
Bushi—Warrior
Bushido—Way of the warrior
Chudan—Middle-level area between neck and waist
Dojo—Place of ways, school
Dojo Kun—The IKA school creed
Domo arigato gozaimashita—Thank you very much
Gedan—Lower level, area below waist
Gosoku Ryu—Soke's hard and fast style
Gyaku—Reverse
Hai—Yes
Hayaku—Quickly
Hayasa—Fast technique execution
Hidari—To the left
Hajime—Begin
Hanmi—Half
Hiki—Pulling
Ipon kumite—Single movement sparring
Jiyu ippon kumite—Freestyle one-step sparring
Jodan—Upper level, area from neck up
Juji—Cross
Kamae—Ready position
Karate—Empty hand
Karateka—One who practices karate
Kata—Form
Katana—Long samurai sword
Ki—Inner strength
Kiai—Loud shout executed at focus point of movement
Kihon—Basic training
Kime—Focus
Ki o tsuke—Attention

Kobudo—Martial arts using weapons
Kokusai Karate Do Kyokai—International Karate Association
Kumite—Sparring
Kyu—Rank, class, grade
Mae—Forward or front
Makiwara—Hard striking pad
Mawatte—Turn
Migi—To the right
Mokuto—Meditation state
Morote—Both hands, double
Nage uke—Reversal or countertechnique
Neko—Cat
Nihon kumite—Double movement sparring
Obi—Belt
Osoku—Low technique execution
Osu—Push and endure, a salutation used in karate
Otagai ni rei—Bow to each other, respect to class
Otori—Throw
Otoshi—Drop
Rei—Salutation
Ryu—Style
Sanbon kumite—Triple movement sparring
Seiken—Fore fist, knuckles of index and middle fingers
Seiza—Proper sitting position
Senpai—Junior instructor
Sensei—Teacher
Shiai—Contest
Shihan—Master teacher
Shomen ni rei—Bow to front, respect to dojo
Shotokan—IKA's foundation style, developed by Gichin Funakoshi
Soke—Creator of art
Soke, Shihan, Sensei, ni rei—Bow to instructor
Soto—Outside
Tai kai—Tournament training
Tsuki—Attack
Tsuru—Crane
Tsuzukete—Continue, fight on
Uchi—Inside
Ukemi—Fall
Ushiro—Backward, rearward
Waza—Technique
Yame—Stop
Yoi—Ready

Yoko—Side
Yukuri—Slowly
Tsukami—Grasp

Parts of the Body
Ago—Chin
Ashi—Foot/leg
Atama—Head
Hiji—Elbow
Hiza—Knee
Kao—Face
Karada—Body
Koshi—Hip
Kubi—Neck
Mata—Thigh
Me—Eye
Mimi—Ear
Nodo—Throat
Saiki—Lower abdomen
Tai—Body
Te—Hand
Tekubi—Wrist
Ube—Thumb
Ude—Arm
Yubi—Finger

Numbers
Ichi—One
Ni—Two
San—Three
Shi—Four
Go—Five
Roku—Six
Shichi—Seven
Hachi—Eight
Ku—Nine
Ju—Ten
Ju + ichi—Eleven
Ju + ni—Twelve
Ni + ju—Twenty
Ni + ju + ichi—Twenty-one
Ni + ju + ni—Twenty-two
Hyaku—One Hundred
Sen—One Thousand
Man—Ten Thousand

Belt Rankings
Colored Belts
10 *kyu*—*Jukyu*—White
9 *kyu*—*Kukyu*—Yellow
8 *kyu*—*Hachikyu*—Orange
7 *kyu*—*Shichikyu*—Blue
6 *kyu*—*Rokukyu*—Purple
5 *kyu*—*Gokyu*—Green, 1st Level
4 *kyu*—*Yonkyu*—Green, 2nd Level

3 kyu—*Sankyu*—Brown, 1st Level

2 kyu—*Nikyu*—Brown, 2nd Level

1 kyu—*Ikkyu*—Brown, 3rd Level

Black Belt

Shodan—1st degree

Nidan—2nd degree

Sandan—3rd degree—Red letters

Yondan—4th degree

Godan—5th degree

Rokudan—6th degree—Red stripe

Shichidan—7th degree—Red on one side

Hachidan—8th degree

Kudan—9th degree

Judan—10th degree—Solid red—Grandmaster

Titles

Sempai—Elder, senior

Kohai—Junior, subordinate

Sensei—Teacher

Shihan Dai—Deputy master

Shihan—Master instructor

So-Shihan—Head master

Kancho—Chief, director

Soke—Founder, creator of the art

Stances

Fudo dachi—Freestyle stance like zenkutsu dachi, but equal weight on each leg with the rear foot turned slightly outward and the back knee bent.

Hachiji dachi—Ready stance. The feet are a shoulder-width apart and the toes are pointed outward.

Hangetsu dachi—Similar to a short front stance with the toes slightly inward. Outward pressure is exerted with the thighs. Longer than Sanchin dachi.

Hanmi zen kutsu dachi—Half-front stance (short).

Hebi dachi—Snake stance, forward movement, zig zag.

Heiko dachi—Feet parallel and a shoulder-width apart.

Heisoku dachi—Feet together stance.

Ippon dachi—Single-leg stance; up on one leg.
Kagato dachi—On the heels of the feet.
Kiba dachi—Horse stance.
Kizami dachi—Sliding forward stance.
Ko kutsu dachi—Back stance.
Kosa dachi—Cross-leg stance.
Mage Tsumasaki Dachi—Stance on toes with the toes folded over.
Musubi dachi—Heels together, toes pointed outward stance (attention).
Neko ashi dachi—Cat stance.
Rei dachi—Short stance, if left foot forward, pointed at 12 o'clock, right at 2 o'clock, heels aligned.
Sanchin dachi—Short stance, toes inward with outward leg pressure, "3 wars stance."
Shiko dachi—Horse stance with toes pointed outward; sumo wrestler stance, "square stance."
Shizen dachi—Natural stance, like hachiji dachi, but more relaxed.
Sokuto dachi—On the balls of the feet.
Suri ashi dachi—Glide step stance.
Tachi kata—Exercise of the various stances.
Tsumasaki dachi—Stance where you are up on your toes.
Uchimata dachi—Shoulder-width, toes pointed inward stance.
Zenkutsu dachi—Front stance.

Strikes

Choku tsuki—Straight punch
Chudan tsuki—Stomach punch
Empi—Elbow attach
Gedan empi—Downward elbow attach
Gedan tsuki—Low punch
Gedan uchi—Downward strike
Giyuku tsuki—Reverse punch

Kakuto—Strike with top of wrist, crane position

Keito—Bottom of wrist downward strike

Haisho—Open hand back of hand strike

Haito—Ridge hand strike, index finger side

Hasami tsuki—Double-scissors strike

Hiraken— Extended knuckle punch

Ipon tsuki—Single extended knuckle punch

Ippon nukite—Single finger thrust attack

Jodan tsuki—Face punch

Kagi tsuki—Hooking punch

Kizami—Lead hand jab

Kentsui—Closed fist downward hammerfist strike

Kumate—Bear claw attack

Mae ate hijiate—Front forearm strike

Mawashi hijiate—Circular forearm strike

Mawashi tsuki—Circular motion punch

Morote tsuki—Double punch

Nukite—Open hand finger thrust attack

Oizuki—Stepping forward lunging punch

Otoshi hijiate—Downward forearm strike

Sei ken—Punch with index and middle knuckles

Shote—Palm heel strike

Shuto—Knifehand strike

Taore otoshi uchi—Takedown strike

Tate tsuki—Vertical fist punch

Teisho—Palm heel strike

Tsuki kata—Exercise of the various punches

Uraken—Backfist strike

Ushiro empi—Elbow attack to the rear

Ushiro hijiate—Rearward forearm strike

Washide—Finger claw strike, fingers together to form a single point

Yama tsuki—Stomach-level uppercut punch

Yoko empi—Side elbow attack

Yoko Hijiate—Side forearm strike

Zuzuki—Head butt

Kicks

Ashi barai—Sweep

Ashibo kake uke—Hooking opponent's leg with your leg

Fumikomi—Stomping heel kick

Giyaku mawashi geri—Reverse roundhouse kick

Haisoku—Kick with the top of the foot

Hiza geri—Kick with knee

Josokute—Kick with the ball of the big toe

Kagato geri—Heel kick

Keage—Snap kick

Kekomi—Thrust kick

Mae geri—Front kick

Mawashi geri—Roundhouse kick

Mikazuki geri—Crescent kick

Nidan geri—Double jump kick

Sankaku tobi geri—Jumping triple kick

Sokuto—Kick with the edge of the foot

Taore geri—Kicking from the ground

Taore kagato uchi—Heel kick from the ground

Tobi geri—Jump kick

Tsumasaki geri—Kick with the toes

Uchi mawashi geri—Inside roundhouse kick

Ura mawashi geri—Hook kick, inside roundhouse

Ushiro geri—Back kick

Yoko geri—Side kick

Blocks

Ashi Nagashi uke—Sweeping block with leg

Ashi no ura uke—Inside leg block

Chudan shuto uke—Knifehand block at stomach level

Chudan uke—Stomach block

Fumikomi ude uke—Thrust kick downward, block with the arm

Gedan shuto uke—Knifehand block below waist level

Haito uke—Block with knifehand, index finger side

Hiza uke—Knee block

Jiuji uke—Double crossing-block

Jodan age uke—Rising block under opponent's arm

Jodan shuto uke—Knifehand block at head level

Jodan uke—Up block

Kaki wake uke—Double block, spreading arms of opponent

Kakuto uke—Wrist block with top of wrist

Keito uke—Wrist block with bottom of wrist

Mikazuki uke—Half-moon sweeping block with hand or foot

Morote sukui—Double scooping block

Morote uke—Double arm block

Fumikomi shito uke—Stomping kick with knifehand block

Nagashi uki—Sweeping arm block

Osoto uke—Inside-to-outside stomach block

Shuto uke—Block with knifehand, little finger side

Sokuto osae uke—Pinning opponent to the ground with bottom of foot

Taisabaki uke—Evasion technique, pushing opponent in the direction of the attack

Teisho ashi uke—Palm heel block to leg

Keito uke—Top of wrist block

Te nagashi uke—Sweeping block

Teo osae uke—Palm heel downward block

Tsuru uke—Crane hand block

Uchi uke—Outside-to-inside stomach block

International Karate Association Honbu No Kata

By Soke Takayuki Kubota — 10th Dan

Gosoku Ryu
Kihon ichi no kata
Kihon ni no kata
Kihon san no kata
Kihon yon no kata
Uke no kata
Ni no kata
Gosoku
Ju hachi no tachi kata
Gosoku yo dan
Denko getsu
Rikyu
Tamashi
Go no kata
Gosoku Godan
Raiden
Anso no kata
Sonota no kata
Kime no kata

Shotokan
Heian shodan
Heian ni dan
Heian san dan
Heian yo dan
Heian go dan
Tekki sho dan
Hangetsu
Basai dai
Kanku dai
Kanku sho
Jion
Jite
Empi
Goju shi o sho
Unsu
Sochin
Sonota no kata

Gosoku Weapons Kata
San kaku giri—Katana
Atemi no kata—Katana
Kubo giri—Katana
Giyaku giri—Katana
Iaido ichi no kata—Katana
Iaido ni no kata—Katana
Iaido san no kata—Katana
Toshin—Katana
Keibo jitsu—Jo
Ken shin ryu—Jo
Washi no kata—Tonfa
Jiuji uke—Tonfa

Tsuye ichi no kata—Cane
Tsuye ni no kata—Cane
Tsuye san no kata—Cane
Tsuye yon no kata— Cane
Tsuye go no kata— Cane
Tsuye roku no kata—Cane
Giyaku tsuye no kata—Cane
Mawashi no kata—Cane
Giyaku mawashi no kata—Cane
Kubotai no kata—Kubotai
So nota no kata

Tai otoshi
Kata hiki otoshi kara
Gaku kata otoshi
Katana Ge
Osae kome
Ashi shime waza
Giyakute waza
Giyaku waza
Kataguruma
Sonota

Kubota Jiu-Jitsu
Mae ukemi
Hidare ukemi
Migi ukemi
Kuruma ukemi
Ushiro ukemi
Nagashi ukemi
Tai sabaki ukemi
Koshi Nage ukemi
Soto gake
Uchi gake
Ipon nage
Hiki nage
Oshi nage
Tomoi nage
Ippon ashi barai
Nihon ashi barai
Kubi hiki otoshi
Kata hiki otoshi
Kubi hiki kara
Giyaku kubinage

Gosoku Ryu Forms, Training Exercises, and Techniques

▲ Yoko geri—Side kick.

▲ Mawashi geri—Roundhouse kick.

▲ Ura mawashi geri—Inside roundhouse kick.

▲ Gyaku mawashi geri—Reverse roundhouse kick.

▲ Yoko fumi komi—Side thrust kick.

▲ Taore mawashi geri—Roundhouse kick from the ground.

▲ Taore fumi age—Side thrust kick from the ground.

▲ Yoko tobi geri—Flying side kick.

▲ Uura gyaku mawashi geri—Inside reverse roundhouse kick.

▲ Ura mawashi ushiro geri—Inside roundhouse kick to the rear.

⚠ Chudan tsuki—Mid-level punch.

⚠ Jodan tsuki—Face-level punch.

⚠ Shuto tsuki—Knifehand strike.

⚠ Nukite—Finger thrust strike.

▲ Haito—Ridgehand strike.

▲ Gyaku jodan tsuki—Reverse punch to the face.

▲ Gyaku gedan tsuki—Reverse punch, lower level.

▲ Shote—Palm heel strike.

▲ Mawashi uchi—Roundhouse punch.

▲ Ken tsui—Hammerfist strike.

◂ Mae empi—Front elbow strike.

▲ Yoko empi —Side elbow strike.

▲ Uchi otoshi empi—Downward elbow strike.

Uke Kata—
Blocking Form

▲ Chudan uchi uke—Mid-level inside block.

▲ Jodan uke—Face-level up block.

▲ Gyaku uke—Reverse block.

▲ Gyaku gedan barai—Reverse down block.

▲ Shote gedan barai—Open-hand down block.

▲ Jodan age uke—Rising up block.

◀ Jodan jiyuji uke—Double up block.

Fighting Karate

▲ Gyaku shote uke—Reverse open-hand block.

▲ Reiote uke—Gosoku Ryu style block.

◀ Uchi otoshi shote uke—Down block with the open hand.

▲ Hiza shote uke—Knee block with the open hand.

▲ Hiza uke—Knee block.

◀ Jiyuji uke—Double down block.

▲ Ushiro gedan barai—Rearward down block.

▲ Mae geri hiza uke—Blocking front kick with knee block.

◄ Gosoku hiza uke—Knee block with an open hand Gosoku Ryu block.

▲ Mae geri nagashi uke—Leg block with sweeping motion.

▲ Mae geri ashi barai uke—Front kick leg sweep.

◄ Ushiro geri tome uke—Rear behind knee block.

▲Ushiro geri fumikomi uke—Rear downward thrust kicking block.

▲Mae geri gyaku nagashi uke—Sweeping reverse hand block against a front kick.

◀Mawashi geri tsukami uke—Catch the roundkick.

⌃Mae geri sokuto uke—Blocking front kick with the bottom of the foot.

⌃Mae geri ashi barai uke—Leg sweeping block against a front kick.

◁Mae geri tsukami—Leg grab defense against a front kick.

Ready position.

Pull belt in mae geri form.

Holding belt from the back.

While holding belt, kick.

Fighting Karate

▲ Ready stance in fudo dachi—Holding from behind.

▲ Pull left shoulder and push hip while punching.

▲ Ready stance—Holding from behind.

▲ Mid-level punch while holding belt from behind.

◢ Holding the belt from the front.

◢ Starting to pull as the trainee punches.

◂ Pull hard on the belt.

▲ Chudan soto uke—Outside block middle level using weights.

▲ Uchi uke—Inside block middle level using weights.

▲ Chudan tsuki—Middle level punch using weights.

▲ Jodan uke and empi uke—Up block and elbow strike using weights.

Fighting Karate

▲ Jodan soto uke and uchi uke—Inside and outside block, upper level.

▲ Ate uke—Hit the attacking arm with the base of the wrist.

▲ Oshi uke—Pushing action done mostly above the elbow joint for better control.

▲ Chudan gyaku tsuki—Mid-level reverse punch with weights.

⌃ Shinai to head for control and focus training.

⌃ Jodan uke exercise—Up block head-level training exercise.

◁ Chudan tsuki exercise—
Mid-level thrusting training.

⋏Lift left and right leg, alternating 10 times on each side.

⋏Front kick left and right leg alternating five times on each side.

◁Mid-level front kick against a person punching to the stomach at same time.

Makiwara and Hammer Training

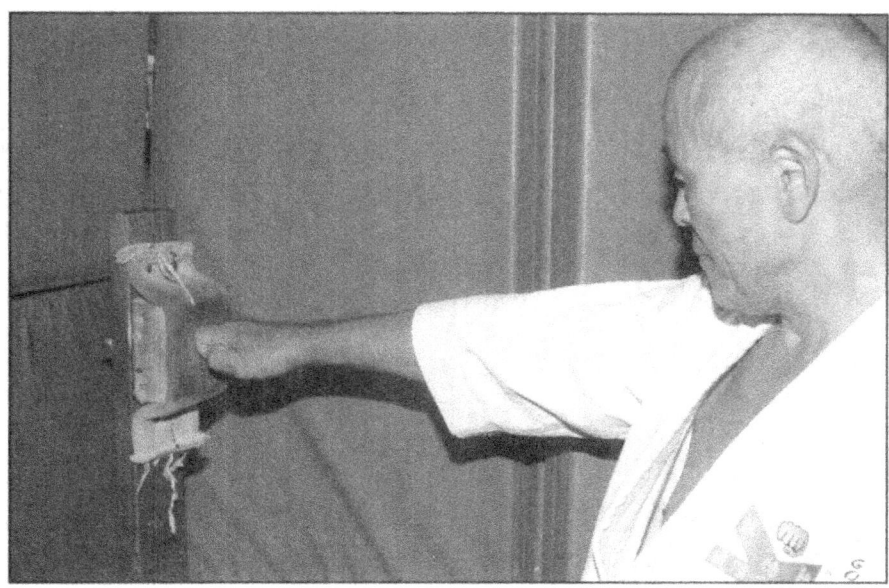

▲ Ippon ken—One-knuckle punch.

▲ Hiraken—Extended knuckle punch.

⊾Hammer (not for everyone—Kubota only).

⊾Hammer strike to the back of the hand.

◁Hammer strike to the shin.

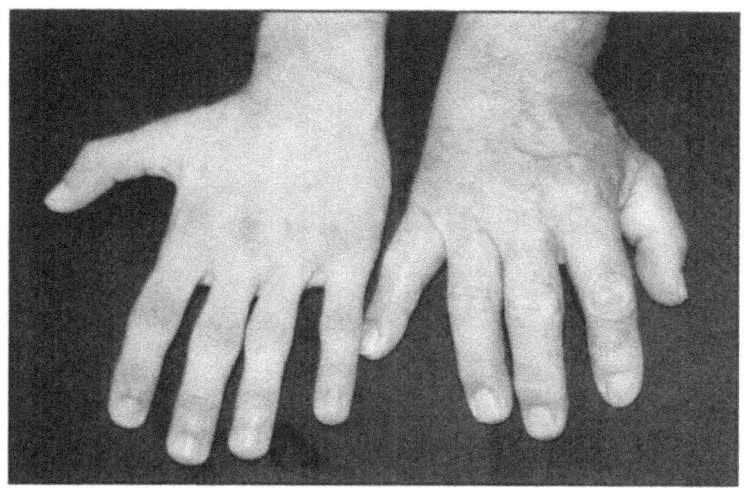

⚘ Kubota hand (right) vs. typical karateka hand.

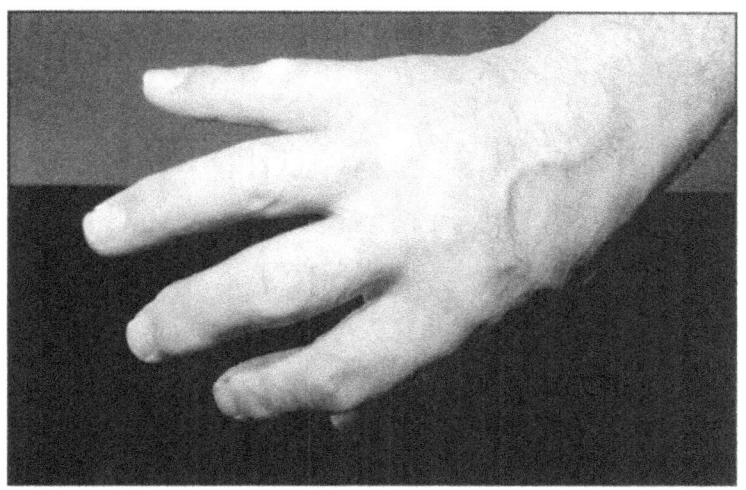

⚘ Kubota hand.

▲ Ready—Soke assumes a cat stance.

▲ Open-hand ready stance.

▲ Same step double block.

▲ Ready.

Fighting Karate

▲ Horse stance ready position.

▲ Rei dachi stance ready position.

▲ Rei dachi stance high-level ready position.

▲ Cat stance ready position.

▲ Fudo dachi stance ready position from head level.

▲ Horse stance, low-level ready position.

▲ Ready position.

▲ Head-level inside block.

Reverse punch counter to face level.

Fighting Karate

◢ Ready position.

◢ Go down on one knee to evade a face-level reverse.

◁ Follow with a reverse punch to the stomach.

⊿ Ready position.

⊿ A jab is blocked to the outside.

◁ Grab the arm, turn your opponent, and reverse punch to the ribs.

Fighting Karate

⌃ Ready position.

⌃ Up block the incoming jab.

⌃ Now block down on the low reverse punch.

⌃ And reverse punch to the face.

▲ Ready position.

▲ A right-hand stomach punch...

▲ ...Is followed by a left-hand face punch.

▲ And a right-hand reverse punch to the ribs.

▲ Ready position.

▲ Sliding in.

▲ A head-level jab is blocked up.

▲ Follow with a reverse punch counter to the stomach.

⊿ Ready position.

⊿ Sliding in.

◁ A step-in punch is stopped with a double block.

Fighting Karate

⋀ The right-hand defense holds punching hand.

⋀ Fire a reverse punch counter to the ribs.

▲ Ready position.

◀ Block with the left hand and grab with the right against a step-in punch.

▲ Knee to the solar plexus.

▲ Now pull the opponent down and smash a left elbow to the back.

Fighting Karate

▲ Ready position.

▲ Slide in.

▲ A jab is met with a left open-hand block.

▲ Inside foot sweep.

⚠ The left hand pulls the head down.

⚠ Reverse punch to the stomach.

Fighting Karate

▲ Ready position.

▲ A double-arm block is used to stop a right-hand, step-in punch.

▲ The right hand pulls the jab down while the left hand jabs to the chin.

▲ Reverse punch to the chest.

▲ Ready position.

▲ A step-in punch.

▲ Evade by dropping to the ground.

Fighting Karate

▲ Apply a roundhouse kick to the groin.

▲ An incoming punch is countered with a right-hand face attack.

▲ The left leg is in and the right leg scissors from behind.

▲ Applying pressure to the back of the knee will buckle the leg.

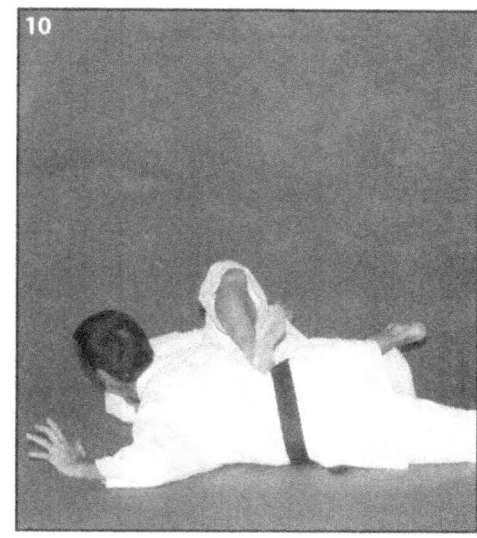

⤴ Heel kick to the kidney or spine.

Fighting Karate

▲ An open-hand inside block stops the incoming jab.

▲ The right hand pushes down to defend against the reverse punch.

▲ Right-hand jab.

▲ A right-hand jab is followed by a left-hand reverse punch.

△ Ready position.

△ A left-hand open-hand block stops the jab.

△ Grab your opponent's shirt.

△ Head butt.

Fighting Karate

▲ Ready position.

▲ Slide in and...

◀ ...Down block the incoming reverse punch.

▲ Grab behind the neck.

▲ Attack with the knee.

Fighting Karate

▲ Ready position.

▲ Double block the incoming jab.

▲ Front sweep while pulling down the left hand.

▲ Hammerfist strike to the back.

▲ Ready position.

▲ Down block the incoming punch.

▲ Grab the wrist.

▲ Thrust kick to the midsection.

Fighting Karate

⌃ Step back and switch stances.

⌃ Now grab the wrist.

⌃ And reverse punch to the face.

▲ Ready position.

▲ Answer with your jab.

▲ Step in and attack with the right elbow.

▲ Focus and follow through with an elbow strike.

Fighting Karate

⌃ Ready position.

⌃ A jumping jab attack...

⌃ ...Is met with a left-hand block.

⌃ Reverse punch on landing.

▲ Ready position.

▲ Stop the reverse punch with an open-hand block.

▲ Turn to prepare for a backkick.

▲ Execute the backkick.

Fighting Karate

▲ Ready position.

▲ Begin with an open-hand block.

▲ The step-in punch is ...

▲ ...Blocked with the leg.

⏶A right jab to the face.

⏴Is followed by a left reverse punch.

Fighting Karate

▲ Ready position.

▲ This is a knee defense against a front kick.

▲ As the opponent steps in, a right-hand block is used.

▲ Switch stances; grab the wrist and elbow attack to the stomach.

▲ Pull the arm down and land an elbow on the back.

Fighting Karate

▲ Ready position.

▲ The opponent slides in.

▲ Step in and jab to the face.

▲ Follow with a reverse punch to the stomach.

⬥ Ready position.

⬥ Go halfway down.

⬥ Now go to the groin and apply a groin kick.

⬥ Get up on your right knee and use a reverse punch to the stomach.

Fighting Karate

Ready position.

Fake a downward attack.

Knock the opponent's hand down.

▲ Jab to the face.

▲ Reverse punch to the stomach.

Fighting Karate

▲ Ready position.

▲ Step in and punch to the stomach.

◀ Reverse punch to the face.

▲ Switch feet.

▲ Reverse punch.

▲ Ready position.

▲ Use the knee as a defense against a punch.

▲ Hammer strike to the face.

▲ Reverse punch to the stomach.

▲ Jab to the face.   ▲ Push the jab into the face.

Fighting Karate

▲ Ready position.

▲ Down block the strike.

◀ Switch feet, raise your right knee and use an open hand to push the strike down. Then bring the knee back.

⬧ Left jab to the face.

⬧ And reverse punch to the stomach.

Fighting Karate

▲ Ready position.

▲ Jab to the face.

◀ Front kick to the stomach.

▲ Use a knifehand to block the strike.

▲ Follow with a reverse punch to the stomach.

Fighting Karate

△ Ready position.

△ Move your left leg inside his front leg for a sweep. Block his strike with an open hand.

◁ Jab to the face.

▲ Ready position.

▲ Step in for an outside leg sweep while pushing out with the open hand.

◀ Fire a reverse punch to the stomach.

Fighting Karate

▲ Ready position.

▲ Take a half-step forward and punch to the face with the right hand.

▲ Switch feet and punch to the face with the left hand.

▲ Follow with a reverse punch to the stomach.

▲ Ready position.

▲ Slide in.

▲ And jab to the face with the left hand.

▲ Raise your left hand to expose the ribs to a reverse punch.

FIGHTING KARATE

▲ Use an elbow attack/defense to chop down on the attacking hand.

▲ Jab to the face with the left hand.

◀ Follow with a reverse hand finger thrust to the throat.

⚐ Ready position.

⚐ Raise your right knee.

⚑ Follow with a double hand sweeping block.

Fighting Karate

⌂ A left-hand jab to the face...

⌂ ...Is followed by a reverse punch to the stomach.

△ Ready position.

△ The right knee is raised.

◁ In anticipation of a front kick to the stomach.

Fighting Karate

▲ Ready position.

▲ As the opponent approaches,

◁ Fire a side thrust kick to the stomach.

⊿ Ready position.

⊿ Jump in.

◁ Slide in and jab to the side of the head.

▲ Now front thrust kick to the stomach.

▲ Add a push kick to keep him off balance.

▲ Ready position.

▲ Take a half-step forward and punch to the face with the left hand.

▲ Step in and front kick with the left.

▲ Add a reverse punch to the stomach.

Fighting Karate

▲ Ready position.

▲ A right snap kick to the stomach,

◁ Is followed by a right thrust kick...

◢...The hand goes back for the wind up.

◢ And a hammer strike to the shoulder.

▲ Ready position.

▲ A right front kick,

▲ Is followed by a left roundhouse.

▲ After blocking with the open hand,

⌃ Step forward and block down.

⌃ Finish with a reverse punch to the face.

Fighting Karate

△ Ready position.

△ First, front kick to the stomach.

△ After defending the lead hand,

△ Fire a backfist to the face.

Ready position.

As the opponent front kicks, move a half-step forward and sweep-block the strike.

Step in and jab to the face.

Slide in with a reverse punch.

▲ Ready position.

▲ A knee stops an incoming backkick.

▲ Pull down from the collarbone,

▲ And hammer strike the chest.

△ Ready position.

△ Slide in to catch the reverse kick.

◁ Grab the leg and reverse punch to the stomach.

▲ Lift and sweep the opponent.

▲ Apply a takedown.

◀ Finish with a punch to the face.

⌃ Ready position.

⌃ Set up your defense for an incoming face kick.

◁ Grab the leg and reverse punch to the stomach.

Fighting Karate

▲ Ready position.

▲ A roundhouse kick is blocked by a double hand sweep.

◀ Attack to the face and stomach simultaneously.

▲ Ready position.

▲ Sweep block the incoming front kick.

◀ Catch the arm of the backfist as it comes in.

FIGHTING KARATE

▲ Use an arm bar takedown and pressure to the biceps.

▲ Finish with an elbow attack to the spine.

▲ Ready position.

▲ Scoop the leg of an incoming front kick.

◁ Counter with an elbow to the neck.

⌂ Ready position.

⌂ As the front kick comes in, scoop the kicking leg.

⌂ Grab his shirt with your right hand.

⌂ Deliver an upward knee to the stomach.

Fighting Karate

▲ Ready position.

▲ Your opponent throws a roundhouse kick.

▲ Duck to evade the kick and simultaneously up block.

▲ When his kick lands, reverse punch to the ribs.

⌃ Ready position.

⌃ Scoop the leg to avoid the front kick.

⌃ Right-hand jab to the face.

⌃ Follow with a left-hand reverse punch to the stomach.

Fighting Karate

⛰ Ready position.

⛰ The opponent slides in and changes sides.

⛰ Use a side up block defense to stop the roundhouse.

⛰ Then counter with a front kick.

▲ Ready position.

▲ Front kick incoming. Use a left-hand down block defense to thwart the front kick.

▲ Switch feet and jab to the face with the right hand.

▲ Fire a left reverse punch to the stomach.

Fighting Karate

▲ Ready position.

▲ The opponent slides in.

▲ Front kick incoming. Use an open-hand sweeping block defense against a front kick and spin the opponent around.

▲ Pull the opponent down by his collar.

⚠ Wind up for a counterattack.

⚠ Now deliver a hammerfist strike to the head or collarbone.

▲ Ready position.

▲ Use a reverse inside block to stop the incoming roundhouse kick.

◁ Grab the leg and counter.

▲ Ready position.

▲ An open-hand reverse block is used to stop an incoming roundhouse kick.

▲ Drop to the ground to evade the kick and use an open-hand block to the outside.

▲ Counter with a roundhouse kick to the groin.

▲ Ready position.

▲ Use the lead leg to block an incoming front kick.

▲ Sweep the kicking leg to the side.

▲ Counter with a front kick to the stomach.

Ready position.

The opponent opens with a backkick. Defend by dodging the kick to the left and moving in to scoop the kicking leg.

Grab the kicking leg with the right hand and place the left hand over your opponent's chest in preparation of a sweep.

Use your left leg to sweep your opponent's ground leg. Finish with a jab to the face.

Fighting Karate

▲ Ready position.

▲ Your opponent shows a front kick.

▲ Drop to the ground to evade the kick.

▲ Counter with a sidekick to the groin.

⚊ Ready position.

⚊ As your opponent shows a backkick, prepare to deliver a counterkick to the back of his leg.

◁ Deliver the punishing counterkick.

FIGHTING KARATE

⚊ Pushing down on the back of the knee drops the opponent. You can then pull him down from behind by grabbing the collar.

⚊ Knifehand strike to the face or collarbone.

▲ Ready position.

▲ Deliver a front kick.

◀ As your opponent counters with a reverse punch, switch feet and down block with your left hand.

⌃Follow with a reverse punch to the stomach with the right hand.

⌃The blocking hand then raises to jab his face.

⌃ Ready position.

⌃ A reverse punch is blocked by a sweeping right leg.

◁ Step in and counter the front kick with your left leg.

▲ Switch feet and apply a double open hand sweeping block.

▲ Finish with a reverse punch to the stomach.

▲ Ready position.

▲ As you deliver a front kick to the opponent, he stops the attack with a down block.

◄ Step in and deliver a backfist.

▲ Connect to the right side of the head.

▲ Follow with a left reverse punch to the stomach.

⚠ Ready position.

⚠ Simultaneously sweep with the right leg and jab to the face.

◁ Follow with a roundhouse punch to the face.

Fighting Karate

▲ Ready position.

▲ Use your front leg to sweep your opponent's front leg.

◄ Step in and front kick to the stomach.

⌂ Step in and jab to the face.

⌂ Follow with a reverse punch to the stomach.

Fighting Karate

▲ Ready position.

▲ Front kick to your opponent's stomach.

▲ Sweep his lead leg.

▲ Turn and prepare to deliver a backkick.

△ Connect on the backkick.

△ Turn and jab to the face.

◁ Then reverse punch to the stomach.

Fighting Karate

▲ Ready position.

▲ Deliver a front kick.

▲ As you fire an inside roundhouse kick, your opponent counters with a sweeping block.

▲ Grab your opponent's hand as he punches.

▲ Turn.

▲ Deliver a backkick.

Fighting Karate

▲ Ready position.

▲ Deliver a front kick.

▲ Now turn.

▲ And deliver a backkick to the stomach.

⌃ Turn and fire a left knifehand strike to the neck.

⌃ Add a right-hand reverse punch to the stomach.

▲Ready position.

▲As the punch comes in, step in and block with the left hand. Then crouch and grab your opponent's groin with your right hand.

◀Lift the opponent on your shoulder.

Fighting Karate

▲ Now throw your opponent down to the ground and prepare to deliver a right-hand punch.

▲ Connect with the punch to the ribs.

◄ Follow with a choking attack.

▲ Ready position.

▲ Your opponent goes down on the ground to deliver a dragon tail sweep.

▲ Step in and block the sweep with your shin.

▲ Counter with a stomping kick to the ribs with your right leg.

Fighting Karate

▲ Ready position.

▲ A sweep is imminent.

◂ As your opponent sweeps your lead leg...

▲...Prepare to fall.

▲ Once on the ground, counter with a thrust kick to the stomach.

Fighting Karate

▲ Ready position.

▲ Your opponent charges.

▲ As your opponent steps in with a punch, block and grab with your left hand and prepare to sweep his lead leg.

▲ Pull down on your opponent's left arm with your left arm. At the same time, lift and sweep the left leg.

As the opponent goes down to the ground, prepare for a right-hand counterattack.

Counter to the stomach with a reverse punch.

Fighting Karate

▲ Ready position.

▲ As the front kick comes in, scoop the leg and grab the shirt with the right hand.

▲ Step in with the right leg and prepare for a sweep takedown.

▲ Place your right leg behind the opponent's ground leg.

▲ Push with the right hand and simultaneously sweep the leg with your right leg.

▲ Your opponent goes to the ground.

▲ Hold your opponent's leg.

▲ Deliver a counterpunch to the stomach.

Fighting Karate

▲ Ready position.

▲ The right leg prepares to sweep.

▲ Sweep the back leg with your right leg.

▲ Once the sweep is complete, push with the left hand, if necessary.

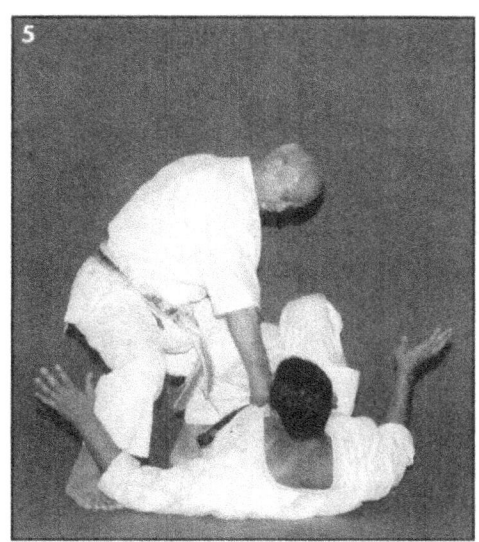

▲ Counter with a right-hand punch to the stomach or....

▲ ...Execute a thrust kick with the edge of foot to the neck.

Fighting Karate

▲ Ready position.

▲ As the front kick comes in, slide in and scoop the kick with your right hand. Simultaneously grab his shirt with your left hand.

▲ Take your opponent down by lifting his leg and pulling his left hand down.

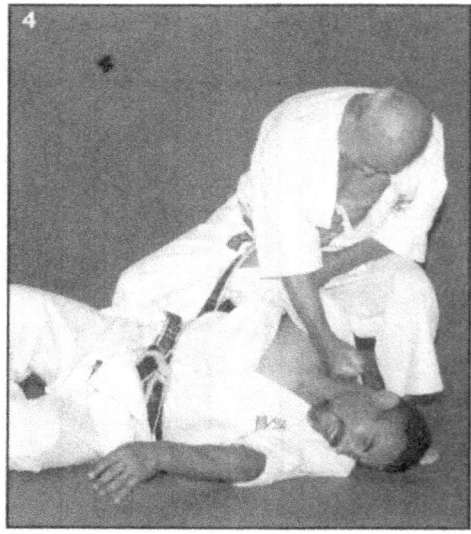

▲ Finish with a right-hand punch to the face.

⌃ Ready position.

⌃ Deliver a jab to the face.

⌃ Turn and prepare to deliver a backkick.

⌃ Apply a roundhouse kick to the ribs or kidney area.

Fighting Karate

⌃ Now step in behind your opponent's leg and perform a sweep takedown. At the same time, push with your right hand.

⌃ The opponent is down and vulnerable to a strike.

◁ Punch to the ribs with your right hand.

▲ Ready position.

▲ As the front kick comes in, scoop the leg with your right hand and grab his shirt with the left.

◀ Pull the opponent to your left using your left hand. At the same time, lift his kicking leg with your right hand.

▲ The opponent hits the ground.

▲ Counter with a punch to the face.

▲ Ready position.

▲ Deliver a jab to the face.

▲ Step in and begin the back leg sweep with your right leg.

▲ Continue the sweep.

Fighting Karate

▲ Reach in and grab the opponent.

▲ Follow through with the sweep while simultaneously pulling the opponent down.

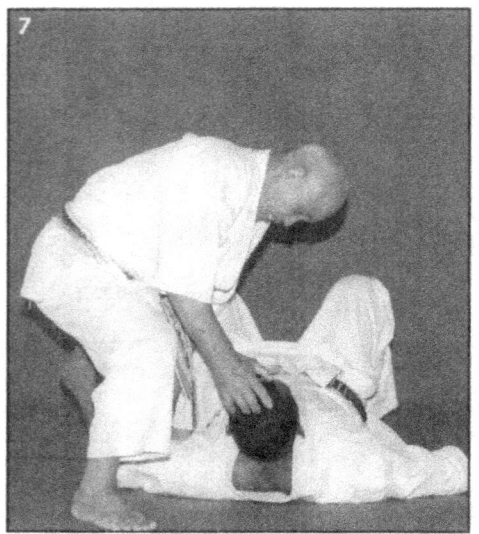

▲ Push the opponent to the ground.

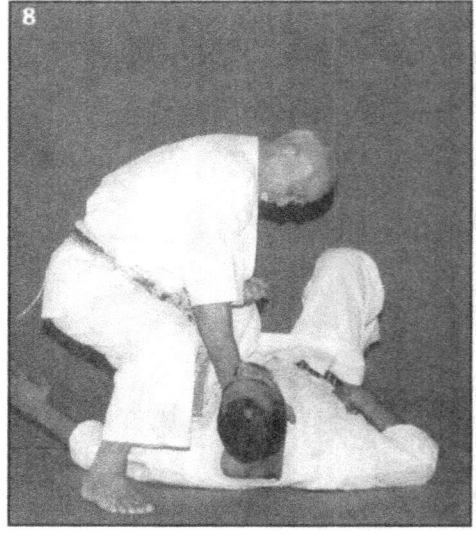

▲ Punch to the stomach.

Ready position.

Prepare to sweep the opponent.

The opponent goes down.

Thrust kick to his face.

IKA Gosoku Ryu Founder and Grandmaster
Soke Takayuki Kubota, 10th Dan

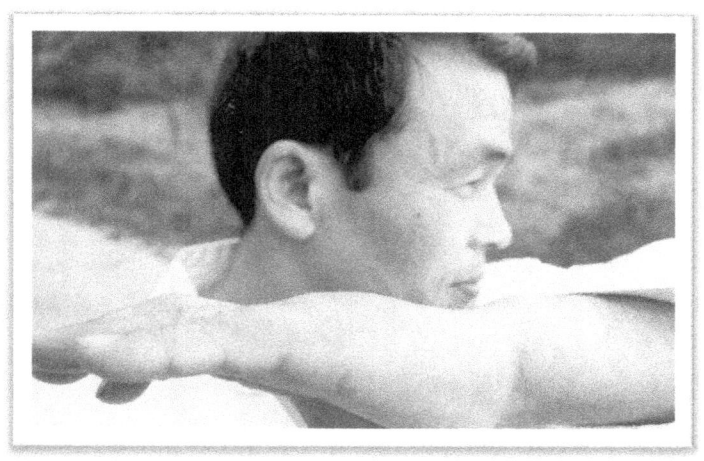

Takayuki Kubota – *"Against the Grain"*

By JOSE M. FRAGUAS

"Bushido, I have found, lies in dying. When confronted with two alternatives, life and death, one is to choose death without hesitation. A man with great valor does not think of the outcome of the fight, he fervently plunges right into the jaws of death..."

– HAGAKURE

TAKAYUKI KUBOTA is one of the most famous and respected karate masters in the world. Born on September 20, 1934, on the Japanese island of Kyushu, the effectiveness of Master Kubota's fighting method started at the Tokyo Police Department, where he was known as "the one-man riot squad." Once in the U.S., he demonstrated and performed his breathtaking strength and conditioning exercises at Ed Parker's Long Beach International Championships in 1966. Many were shocked by these demonstrations that captured the attention not only of students but other well-known karate masters as well.

In addition to teaching his very aggressive style of Gosoku Ryu karate, Sensei Kubota has been acknowledged as the most active and innovative karate instructor in the field of law enforcement techniques. Although his hair has grayed some since his memorable Long Beach demonstration, he still leads his classes with the same intensity and dedication he did then. He was brave enough to incorporate technical modification at a time when this approach to traditional karate was strongly criticized. He stood for what he believed and based on his sense of functionality, he developed one of the most efficient styles of karate known today.

In the candid interview that follows, Master Kubota gives us his thoughts and ideas on his development and teaching of the Gosoku Ryu Karate style.

When did you start training?

"During World Word II, many Okinawans came to my home in Kyushu and my family helped some of them. Two of these men were experts in *to-de* (it was not called karate in Okinawa at that time) and taught the townspeople in return for their assistance. Their names were Terada and Tokunaga. When I was only 4 years old, my father began to teach me the very basics of karate do – *kihon*, *kata* and a lot of *makiwara* training. My training was very hard; everything evolved around the number 500: 500 kicks, 500 punches, 500 stance changes, 500 hits to the makiwara, and 50 minutes of kata. Every day was very much the same. My father was teaching me karate to fight to kill, not for self-improvement or sport but for war. We had no karate-gi to wear after the war, but it didn't matter; we just trained very, very hard for real fighting. That is the way karate was taught in those days. Later on, I moved on to Master Kanken Toyama's dojo. Toyama Shihan was a direct student of Yasutsune Itosu and Kanryo Higashionna."

What happened when you moved to Tokyo?

"I began teaching karate a couple of years after I arrived there. At the time, there were few other instructors teaching, but we always had a good relationship helping each other out and getting together for technical exchanges."

What style do you teach?

"I teach Gosoku Ryu karate. My teaching is based on how to use power when power is the answer, how to use speed when speed is the answer, and how to use evasion when evasion has to be used. Nothing will work all the time under all kind of circumstances. You need to have all the physical and conceptual elements, but intelligence also, in order to combine them efficiently."

When and how did you decide to develop the Gosoku Ryu style?

"Let me tell you first of all that we practice Shotokan kata for the basics. I developed Gosoku Ryu when I was in Japan because, after training under different instructors, I realized at an early stage that the Shotokan style that I learned in those years was very much "unidirectional." Then, after meeting other masters, like Gogen Yamaguchi, I thought that some other "circular" elements should be added to that Shotokan foundation. I started more and more to analyze the actual combat and brought into a new system, other important aspects that made the fighting aspect of my karate more complete, and that were necessary. Of course, this approach is normal today, and even the old JKA style of karate is not like it used to be in the '50s and '60s, but when I did these modifications, I definitely was going *against the grain*."

Did you get any resentment from other masters?

"I know some of them thought I was doing something wrong. They never told me to my face, but I know they thought that way. What is interesting is to note that 20 years later, they started to do the same thing to their styles. The difference is that I changed the name of what I was doing because it was not the original style I learned. I had to be honest and call it differently. That is how Gosoku Ryu was born."

You never capitalized on who your teachers were in order to get recognition. Why?

"Because I don't believe in doing that. Your skill in karate is not passed to you because your instructor is well known or famous. I have seen many people telling everybody who their teacher was…but that is irrelevant if you can't deliver. Just because my teacher was very famous doesn't mean that I know what I am doing. Karate is up to you. You are the one who must deliver…not your teacher. So what is the point in telling everybody about who-and-who is your teacher? To validate you and your school? The only one who can validate what you do as karate-ka is yourself, not your teacher's name and reputation."

Do you teach karate in the traditional way or have you made some changes?

"Of course, I made changes. It is not that I have changed the basic techniques but, since I have studied different styles, I understand their strong and weak points. For instance, some karate styles are very good at offensive maneuvers but they lack an extensive repertoire in defensive actions. In Gosoku Ryu, I have incorporated many different methods."

Why do you have so many foreign students training in your Glendale dojo?

"I guess it became almost a tradition. They are students of other top instructors in different karate styles as Shotokan, Goju Ryu, Shito Ryu, etc., in their own countries. I think they are attracted by the versatility of what I teach. I honestly don't know the main reason, though. What I do is provide them with the best training and welcome them. I believe this is great in many ways. You can find here students from France, Italy, Hong Kong, Mexico, Korea, and more – it's like visiting the United Nations."

Do you think all those students from other styles come to you in order to overcome the flaws in their own systems?

"I don't know. It is true that some styles have weak points and when the student reaches the black belt level, he might see those, so he decides to go out and train in a different style. Some styles are very strong, but they are weak in defense. Other are very fast but lack stamina."

Your students are very successful in sport karate. Do you teach special techniques for competition?

"Yes, I do, but they are successful because they train hard and put a lot of time into it. What's funny is that a lot of them are very good at getting disqualified for attacking too hard. Competition techniques don't work in real life and in self-defense situations because the whole environment is different – but being a professional instructor means giving people what they want and need."

So, you try to give each student what he or she is looking for?

"Yes. That's why in my dojo you can see movie stars, film directors, lawyers, undercover agents, and even street fighters. I believe that a good instructor has to be able to teach every component of his art at every level. You can't teach a child in the same way you teach an undercover agent."

Do you think that different karate styles competing against each other will lead karate to a modification of technique?

"That is exactly what is happening now; it's what I saw many years ago and I incorporated into Gosoku Ryu. They will have to analyze others styles and find about their own strong and weak points to try overcome them. It also will affect kata performance, since Shotokan people might be doing Shito Ryu or Goju Ryu kata if the kata their practitioners have selected for competition has its roots in other "ryu." We know many well-known Shotokan masters teaching Shito and Goju katas to their black belts these days. I was not "crazy" when I said 30 years ago what eventually was going to happen. Little by little, the styles will be modified."

Do you think these masters eventually will change the original styles?

"It is one thing is to "change" the style and another to incorporate or to add elements from other karate styles. For instance, Master Hirokazu Kanazawa is a straight Shotokan teacher, but he not only personally trained in Goju and Shito but also teaches Goju and Shito katas to his students, because he knows these specific katas have a value to be added to the Shotokan principles. Unfortunately, he was criticized when he started, but today everybody understands and respects him for openly doing that. It is only fair to accept the fact that 20 years from now the styles, no matter how traditional, will be different from what they are now."

How do you train students for competition?

"I take them to as many competitions as possible to match them against different karate styles. I make them train harder to discover their weak points while they are under pressure and correct them. This is what I call "closing the gaps." Eventually, as they get smarter, all these mistakes will fade away, and they will become instinctive fighters. However, it is very different to be a fighter than a competitor. You have to watch the students in the artificial competition atmosphere. Then, after seeing the weak points they expose during matches, we go back to the dojo and work on producing good competition fighters."

Do you have any favorite techniques?

"I like sweeping and counter-punching a lot, but I don't really prefer any one technique. You need different techniques because people are different – and you need to have tools to deal with different kinds of opponents. This is the reason why it is so important to spar against many different stylists."

Do you have any objection to sport karate?

"I don't think there's anything wrong with competition. What I really dislike is that it is very limiting as far as technique is concerned. And that is bad. I believe that there should be a lot more techniques and not only *gyaku tsuki* and *mae geri*. This is the reason for the poor attendance at karate competitions."

Do you feel karate will go the same way as judo?

"If we keep doing the things this way, for sure. A long time ago, they started to create rules for judo until judo was not a martial art anymore. To prevent this from happening to karate, we must have a widening of techniques, and not prohibit so many practical moves that exist in the art and allow the students and competitors to use them."

You shocked everybody at Ed Parker's International Karate Championship in 1966 when you beat your own hand with a sledgehammer.

"I believe that in order to deliver or take a punch, the practitioner has to be strong. I've always trained like this, but I don't push it on anyone else. I will teach it if someone wants to learn, but a lot of it is mental training, too."

How important is the physical body conditioning you do in the complete context of the art of karate?

"To win a sport competition, you don't need it. Now, if what you are training is Budo karate, you must condition your body to become a weapon. I am not the only one who advocates that philosophy. Many others do. Master Morio Higaonna from Okinawa is a good example. He does a hard body conditioning. His hands, feet, fingers, etc., are karate weapons. That is important to keep in mind. In order for your technique to be effective, your body must be capable of deliver it hard without hurting yourself and inflicting the maximum amount of damage. That's real karate."

Why did you start to do this kind of demonstrations?

"When I came to America, only the style of Shotokan was known to the public. Sensei like Tsutomu Ohshima were here and others like Hidetaka Nishiyama and Teruyuki Okazaki were in the country teaching this style. Goju Ryu was not that well-known but because of the charismatic Gogen "The Cat" Yamaguchi, people were curious about it. So, in order to bring attention to the style of Gosoku Ryu, I had to do things that nobody else was doing and breaking was what really caught the people's attention."

How did you get involved with this kind of training?

"My teacher told all the students that we must toughen our bodies and make them strong so we could attack anyone. I remember we had no makiwara at all, so we used rocks. I recall hitting one wrong and cutting my hand pretty badly. My teacher came and did what he thought would help me the most – he poured salt in the open cuts."

So, you believe in *makiwara* training?

"If you are in a real fight with a big opponent, you have to be strong, and you need a lot of power to be able to stop him properly. In the old karate tradition, you had to kill him before he killed you. I like that kind of training. I teach two different styles of hitting the *makiwara*. First you must hit it relaxed and focus on the surface; I call this the "stopping style." The next method is to carry the strike through. You must make the entire body a weapon – even your toes."

What about your special hammer training?

"I do special concrete training and hammer training; I have done this for a long time. I pound my hands, arms, and shins with a two-pound hammer – this makes you very strong. Back in Tokyo, I was good friends, in my younger days, with Mas Oyama and the famous pro wrestler Rikadozan. We used to train a lot on the makiwara. In fact, when Master Oyama published his first book, he decided to use my picture – but only my hand. He didn't want to use my face. Maybe I wasn't good looking enough."

It has a lot to do with mental training?

"Yes. I believe it is the best way to train. It makes you tough and allows you to develop the true martial arts spirit. You have to overcome the pain and the fear and go beyond the physical. Of course, I use certain criteria to decide whether or not I will teach a student these special methods. They must toughen their bodies, and the best way is through these exercises.

How you start the student into the program?

"He starts out slowly and gradually builds up. After a year, the student can punch the makiwara more than 1,000 times without a problem. Of course, sometimes we have injuries. People don't train like they should and make mistakes, such as hitting the object improperly and breaking their bones. Unfortunately, it comes with the training. It happened to me many times."

Do you think these programs are beneficial for the average practitioner?

"I don't train so I can go to a tournament and do a show. I do it because I want to train my body so I will be prepared for any confrontation. That's the philosophy of my style. You can hit me anywhere you want, and it probably will hurt you more than it does me. The program prepares you to take on anything. At this point, I can block a kendo stick with my forearm and sustain no injury."

What is the most important factor in training students?

"There's no simple answer to that. It depends on the student. Some people improve very fast while others need more time to learn the same material. There are guys that will never become good, but they really enjoy the training because it improves their health and therefore their lives. The bottom line is that they need a good teacher. But, be careful, because a good karate man may be not a good karate teacher."

How important is the length of time a person trains?

"It is paramount. The student may have timing, speed, technique, etc., but after a few minutes against a good opponent, technique goes out the window. It's only after at least ten years of training, when a student's body has absorbed the techniques, and the mind is free to work instinctively on fighting rather than thinking about every move, that you really can be a karate fighter. It takes ten years to produce a mature karate student."

What would be your message for all karate practitioners?

"That they practice the art as a whole through kata, kumite, and kihon. Today, many people train kata and kumite as if they were two different things. Actually, kumite starts with kata, and kata starts with kumite. This mindset would vastly improve any student's kumite. I don't mean the kind of kumite you see now, but the kumite using other techniques like *enpi* (elbow) and *hiza* (knee)."

But that's very dangerous.

"Everything is dangerous if you can't control it. That's why you have to study kata for timing and control. Only if we do this will karate grow and avoid the same pitfalls and fate as judo. Kata allows you to improve your kumite, but you need to know and understand how it does it."

Do you like the way karate has developed in the West?

"I really like the Japanese karate style, but I also understand that different cultures have different ways of approaching the same subject. It is impossible to regulate the whole karate world, but it is not impossible is to teach respect to the students – respect and etiquette. Unfortunately, many dojos in the West lack this. This should be preserved and passed down for future generations. Without respect and etiquette, karate is just common street brawling."

Meditation is an important aspect of your personal training. Do you teach it to your students?

"Yes. I don't tell my students to "leave their mind empty" because that is impossible. This is nonsense. There always will be something in your mind, even the thought of keeping it empty. That is why I developed Anso No Kata, which basically is a form of "meditation through movement." We all undergo trial at different times of our life and, as a sensei, when my students go through these challenging trials, I want to make sure they come out at the other end – not just coming out whole but surfacing as a better person."

You seem to be in excellent relationship with all other masters. How do you do that in a world where egos and politics are all around?

"First of all, I don't think what I do is better than any other style per se…so I don't put down others. This is a way of respecting other masters and styles. Therefore, they do the same for me. Since the very first days in America, and I should say in Japan when I was young too, I always have been a very straightforward person. In Karate, I believe in "can you use it?" If you do many things but when it comes to the moment of being able of use it, you can't, then you have to reevaluate what you are doing. The final test is the actual combat. And that is Budo. That is the mentality we always have to keep in the back of our heads. We can do many things, sports, health, fitness, etc., but at the end of the day, the question is: *Can you fight?*

Martial arts through centuries were expressions of man's basic instinct of survival. There is an important quote from the book *Hagakure – The Book of Samurai* by Yamamoto Tsunemoto that epitomizes the mental spirit a warrior needs to be effective: fearless with total commitment."

You have a very easy-going attitude for being one of the most well-known karate masters in the world.

"Why shouldn't I?"

Any final word?

"If you truly expect to realize your dreams, you should forget the need for blanket approval. If conforming to everyone's expectations is your number one goal, you have sacrificed and lost your uniqueness, and therefore your excellence."

www.ingramcontent.com/pod-product-compliance
Lightning Source LLC
Chambersburg PA
CBHW081743100526
44592CB00015B/2283